In D
When Words Fail
Voice of Jesus
Pray for Me

*A Guide to Praying the Words of Jesus
Through the Holy Scriptures of the Bible*

Melissa McLaughlin

In Dark of Night When Words Fail
Voice of Jesus Pray For Me
Copyright© 2018 by Melissa McLaughlin
Published by Melissa McLaughlin
ISBN-13: 978-0692155875 (Melissa McLaughlin)
ISNB-10: 0692155872

Cover artwork and design by Tom McLaughlin.

Dedicated to my children, Shannon, Laurel and Chris.
May you always hear the Voice of Jesus
in the eternal words of the Bible.

Contents

1. Foreword... 7
2. Introduction... 9

Section One – Where and Why?
3. Where do I find the Voice of Jesus?.................... 17
4. Voice of Jesus in Father, Son and Holy Spirit..... 21
5. Where do I begin?..................................... 23
6. Why the Bible?.. 23
7. Why Jesus?.. 28

Section Two – What's Next? Prepare
8. Prepare ~ What do I need?............................ 35
9. Create a Haven of Time/Schedule/Regularity...... 36
10. Create a Haven of Space............................. 37
11. Which Version of the Bible?......................... 39
12. Where Do I Start Reading in the Bible?............. 40

Section Three – What's Next? Listen and Write
13. Listen and Record from Bible Reading........... 45
14. What Should My Scripture Prayer Include?....... 49
15. Writing Prayers Using Scripture.................... 51
16. Sample Scripture Prayer............................. 53

Section Four – What's Next? Pray
17. Pray with Your Body, Mind and Spirit............ 59
18. Pray Aloud the Words of Jesus...................... 63
19. How Much Time is Needed?........................ 65
20. Closing "The Gift of Pain"......................... 69
21. Acknowledgements................................... 73

FOREWORD

It has often been said, "Pain is not a matter of *if* but a question of *when*". As I read this carefully crafted and spirit-boosting prayer guide, the words of Melissa McLaughlin (Missy) invite me page after page to concede afflictions are certainties and no one on earth is immune to pain, heart-wrenching pain that at times leaves the sufferer speechless and wordless. Any song, poem, novel, or movie attuned to the human condition can confirm the above diagnosis—this book is no exception. Yet what makes this guide stand out is the solution or remedy to which it points:

There is great hope because pain points the sufferer to a High Priest—Jesus—who empathizes with human sorrow and relates to humanity in every way.

Why does my heart resonate so much with the message of Missy's prayer guide?

Well, I am no stranger to pain. In less than 20 months, I lost my dad to a brain aneurysm, a brother to a fatal abduction, another brother to a heart attack, and a sister to triple negative breast cancer. That was the cake. The icing with the cherry on top came a year and a half later when my youthful mom died from uterine cancer. It was a long, dark season of unspeakable grief and soul weariness in my life.

Prone to severe depression, I would not have survived that season had it not been for the grace of God through Christian friends like Missy who pointed me to the ministry of Christ and reminded me of His gentle voice singing over me,

> I ache with you
> I weep with you.

In Dark of Night, When Words Fail summons readers to bring their burdens to Jesus, the One who is well acquainted with grief, and to be heartened by "His powerful yet gentle voice as He prays not *around* the pain but *through* it", according to Missy. With succinct and clear explanations, it provides valuable instructions regarding how Bible-centered prayer works. I invite the reader to join me in taking this prayer journey alongside Missy as we grow more inspired and encouraged by words such as these:

"Though You have made me see troubles, many and bitter, you will restore my life again; from the depths of the earth You will bring me up. You will increase my honor and comfort me once more."
Psalm 71:20-21, *NIV*

In Christ's love,

Louima Lilite

INTRODUCTION

The tears streamed down my cheeks as I listened to his labored breathing. Each breath, a desperate gasp for life. He licked his quivering lips and moaned softly. I brought a cup of water, but he could only take a tiny sip. I was torn, not wanting his life to end, yet praying for his release from pain, pleading for this endless train of suffering to reach its final stop. Still he breathed, still he moaned, still his heart beat. His once vibrant body now disfigured and filled with disease. Each movement brought a new torrent of pain. Death was waiting, but waiting too long. Lurking around the corner, but unwilling to show itself and end this unbearable agony. How long, oh God? How long? How long must we wait in this place of sorrow and pain?

Long past the point of no return, he breathed his last. The warmth left his body and his presence left my life. I expected the heaviness in my heart to lift, but strangely the blanket of sadness clung to me like damp clothes after a walk in the pouring rain. Though I had escaped the sorrow of watching him suffer, now I was left with the sorrow of his absence. An unfillable void, an empty place in my life, an irreplaceable loss, like a priceless porcelain heirloom shattered into pieces on the floor. Though his pain was now gone, so too was his life. When, oh God, when will this train of suffering come to an end?

~~~ * ~~~

Thump, thump, thump. The nervous pounding of my own heart drowned out the chatter of patients and nurses passing by in the hallway. I sat in the exam room waiting for the doctor to make his rounds, gazing numbly at the medical posters on the wall attempting to distract myself with a deluge of medical facts. There was a firm knock on the exam room door. The doctor entered greeting me with a guarded smile. In a soft and serious voice, he explained the outcome of my test results. His recommendations were a blur flooding my mind. Terminal? Permanent? Unwanted choices? Undesirable outcomes? Limited time, limited functioning? My thoughts racing, circling, questioning. What was he saying? This was not possible. This was not me. This must be a dream, a very bad dream. God, others have been healed. Why won't You heal me?

~~~ * ~~~

We waited for the news, but it never came. Praying and praying and praying for a baby. After being married for so long, our hearts' greatest desire was to share our love and our home with our own precious child. Surrounded on every side by family, friends and neighbors who were joyfully toting infants and toddlers on their hips, swapping stories of sleepless nights and baby food sales, we watched and listened from afar with empty arms, aching hearts and a silent home. Instead of toys and diapers strewn about in chaotic loving mayhem, we stared blankly at the cobwebs of our life, a lonely array of tumbleweeds drifting aimlessly back and forth. Where was God? How could it be that the Creator of life, could not create a baby inside of me?

~~~ * ~~~

The hunger pangs rattled my rib cage. I stole another glance at the slight bodies seated near me. The children in this poverty-stricken country had walked a great distance in order to participate in the missionary sponsored program where we now sat together. In my mind's eye, I pictured their small homes along the roadsides of this community. Houses pieced together with great ingenuity using the scant resources available. Pieces of scrap metal for a roof, branches gathered from nearby trees for a porch, small backyard gardens lovingly tended by worn, calloused, bare hands. Why should these little ones seated near me walk home hungry, when people all over the world at this same moment were throwing away food that didn't suit their tastes or their moods, trashing food no longer needed because their plates were still overflowing when the meal ended? How could we live in a world where people with an abundance of food look away to avoid the eyes of hungry children? How did we come to this, pretending not to see? Why doesn't God do something?

~~~ * ~~~

Words? At times like these there are no words. Only fragmented thoughts tossed to and fro by thundering emotions. Each of us has our own dark night of the soul, when no word, phrase, poem, story or song can adequately capture the depth of the soul's sorrow or express the heart's raw cry about this unwanted, uncalled for dark twist in the road, this gut-wrenching moment in time, this lonely, empty place where you now stand. You find yourself voiceless and too paralyzed to pray. As far as the eye can see in a long stretch up ahead lie emptiness, void and sorrow. Miles of brokenness. The ground, gray and dusty beneath your feet. The only sound, a hollow drum beating in your soul. Voices long silent.

Images and feelings swirl through your mind like a tempest with no end, no clear thoughts to arrange into words. Merely groans and sighs too deep for words. The only place left to turn is to God, but the connection to God seems lost, the frequency cut off, the cell tower knocked out. Words? The words fail, falling silent into the deep abyss of your chest. God is your only hope, but all hope seems lost.

In dark of night when words fail, Voice of Jesus, pray for me.

Jesus is calling. Listen for His Voice, feel His heart, look for the song He is singing over you.

The Lord your God is with you, he is mighty to save. He will take great delight in you, he will quiet you with his love, he will rejoice over you with singing.
Zephaniah 3:17

Section One

Where and Why?

SECTION ONE – WHERE AND WHY?

Where do I find the Voice of Jesus?

Jesus, yes, Jesus. How do I find the Voice of Jesus? Where do I begin? Jesus, the Son of God, the Holy One, the only One who loved humanity so much, He sacrificed His own glorious life to pay the penalty for my dirt, my rebellion and my sins. Jesus, the One who arose from the grave and lives now reigning forever in heaven. Jesus, the One who invites every single person into the eternal family of God, if only we believe in Him, confess Him as Lord and surrender our lives to Him. Jesus, the One who sends His Holy Spirit to fill us, lead us and comfort us as we journey through this life.

Jesus, yes, Jesus. There's no doubt about Jesus. Jesus, Creator of my soul. Jesus, Lover of my soul. Jesus, Savior of my soul. Surely Jesus can help, but where do I find Him? How do I hear the Voice of Jesus?

Jesus is calling. Listen for His Voice in the one and only place it can be found, in the pages of the Bible from the first page to the last. From the beginning to the end, the Presence of Jesus is woven into each part of the Bible.

The Son is the image of the invisible God, the firstborn over all creation. For in him all things were created: things in heaven and on earth, visible and invisible, whether thrones or powers or rulers or authorities; all things have been created through him and for him. He is before all things, and in him all things hold together. Colossians 1:15-17

In the beginning was the Word, and the Word was with God, and the Word was God. He was with God in the beginning. Through him all things were made; without him nothing was made that has been made. In him was life, and that life was the light of all mankind. The light shines in the darkness, and the darkness has not overcome it. John 1:1-5

The Bible is the sole source of Jesus' life and Words. The Bible is truth, pure and never changing. The Bible is a story of grand proportions spanning thousands of years, including various genres, involving countless people, places and events. Despite the number of writers, despite the number of years in the telling, the Bible remains one book with only one theme: Jesus. The Bible foretells the coming of Jesus, details the life of Jesus and reveals our future with Jesus. The Bible is the one sure means by which we can discover and encounter the Voice of Jesus for ourselves. The Bible, God's Eternal Truth, God's Word, God's love story, God's communication with humankind from before all time, into the present time and continuing throughout all eternity. The Bible gives an account of God's plan of redemption for all who are willing to hear and receive. The Bible reveals God's heart for creating, loving, teaching and saving humanity starting with the story of Creation and concluding with the announcement of the future return of Jesus. The Bible is God's Word, a glimpse into God's Mind, a love letter from God's Heart given as a gift, a sacred, holy and beautiful gift. The Bible, the Holy scriptures, the words, phrases, verses, stories and songs that tell us of our Creator God, our Savior King Jesus and our Holy Spirit Counselor.

In this prayer guide, the Bible is not argued against, but revered, treasured and uncovered with deepest honor and respect, as we stand in the light of a Holy God, who is completely pure, righteous and just. This same God is also full of love, mercy and kindness. A just God, who because of His own purity cannot say that our "wrong is right". A good Father who must eradicate any evil in His sight, or the good ceases to be good. At the same time a loving God, who invites us to draw near despite our sinfulness and desperate lack of holiness and goodness. A God who maintains justice by requiring the just payment, asking Someone to pay the price for our sins. A God who demonstrates love by asking His own sinless Son to bring about that justice by taking our sins upon Himself, dying on a cross in our place. Jesus Christ, the Son of God, the perfect sacrifice for all of humanity's sin. What amazing love! What amazing grace! Even more, what incredible joy that God's story doesn't end there! Jesus arose from that grave and is now seated at the right hand of the throne of God in the heavenly realms, where all who believe in Him may join Him someday and rejoice together for all eternity!

Voice of Jesus in Father, Son and Holy Spirit

Anchoring this prayer guide are the Christian truths found in the Bible, which recognize God as our Sovereign Creator and Loving Father, Jesus as His one and only Son who died in our place to pay the penalty of justice for our sins and the Holy Spirit who is the very Spirit of God sent to live and move in the hearts of all who believe in Jesus. The Trinity – Father, Son and Holy Spirit. Three parts, One God. Although Father, Son and Holy Spirit are separate, they are yet one and so Father, Son and Holy Spirit are used interchangeably within this book. The Voice of Jesus then, can be heard in the scriptures that refer to God the Father, Jesus Himself and the Holy Spirit.

Jesus answered, "Don't you know me, Philip, even after I have been among you such a long time? Anyone who has seen me has seen the Father. How can you say, 'Show us the Father'? Don't you believe that I am in the Father and that the Father is in me? The words I say to you are not just my own. Rather it is the Father, living in me, who is doing his work. Believe me when I say that I am in the Father and Father is in me; or at least believe on the evidence of the miracles themselves." John 14:9-11

But the Counselor, the Holy Spirit, whom the Father will send in my name, will teach you all things and will remind you of everything I have said to you. (Jesus) John 14:26

There are a host of books that question every detail related to Christ. This is not one of them. The intent of this guide is not to dispute Christian beliefs, but to take hold of them with greater fire, to cling to them in the depths of one's soul, to cast aside everything but the Voice of Jesus as written in the Bible. This book is designed to help you invite the Words and Voice of Jesus into your prayers when the sorrows of this life are so great that they render one silent, when tears seem your only voice, when words fail. By leaning hard into the Bible and asking the Holy Spirit to teach you, the Voice of Jesus can be heard more clearly as you grant His Words and Voice full access to your heart. His Voice then flows through your heart straight into the heart of God joining you together in intimate communion. The One who loves you like no other visits with you, His beloved child. This opens the door of your heart to the Presence of God, a comfort and shelter, a hiding place where you are safe in the everlasting arms, nestled close under His wings of love. Rest and linger long amidst God's Voice of love in the words of the Bible. Let the Lover of your soul hold you there in the deepest part of your heart. As deep calls unto deep.

Deep calls to deep
  in the roar of your waterfalls;
all your waves and breakers
  have swept over me.
Psalm 42:7

Where do I begin?

You have the need. You have the desire. You have Jesus and your heart cries for Him. Now what? Where do you begin? How do you use the Bible to hear the Voice of Jesus and invite Him to pray through you and for you? Let's begin by first answering a few questions.

Why the Bible?

We did not create ourselves. It is God who created us. Rather than asking, "Who am I?" instead let us ask ourselves, "Whose am I?" We belong to Him, we are His creation. As we come to a more profound understanding that from dust we were made and to dust we will return, likewise we begin to more fully comprehend that compared to an eternal God, our lives and our words are both very short-lived. The words of humankind are but a vapor in the wind, like shifting sands beneath our feet. In contrast to this, though written through the hands of human writers, the Holy scriptures of the Bible, are inspired by God and contain His power, His breath, His sovereignty, His thoughts, His Eternal Truth.

Know that the Lord is God. It is he who made us and not we ourselves; we are his people the sheep of his pasture. Psalm 100:3

"For my thoughts are not your thoughts, neither are your ways my ways," declares the Lord. "As the heavens are higher than the earth, so are my ways higher than your ways and my thoughts than your thoughts." Isaiah 55:8-9

All Scripture is God-breathed and is useful for teaching, rebuking, correcting and training in righteousness, so that the servant of God may be thoroughly equipped for every good work.
2 Timothy 3:16-17

Our words are here today and gone tomorrow, but the Bible, the Word of God, lasts for all eternity and calls to us from the Ancient of Days with a power that resounds from before time, speaking of mysteries beyond our understanding. The more we immerse ourselves in the Bible, the more we can hear the Voice of Jesus speaking through His Word, into our hearts and minds. The more we read the Bible, the more our hearts are receptive to His Voice. Our spiritual ears are more finely tuned to His frequency and new rooms of our hearts are opened for Jesus to move in and transform us. As we take in more of the Bible, Jesus can further reveal Himself to us, as our heart relinquishes its own space for Him to reside more readily, more deeply, more completely within.

Heaven and earth will pass away, but my words will never pass away. (Jesus) Matthew 24: 35

The grass withers and the flowers fall, because the breath of the Lord blows on them. Surely the people are grass. The grass withers and the flowers fall, but the word of our God stands forever. Isaiah 40:7-8

Do not think that I have come to abolish the Law or the Prophets; I have not come to abolish them but to fulfill them. I tell you the truth, until heaven and earth disappear, not the smallest letter, not the least stroke of a pen, will by any means disappear from the Law until everything is accomplished. (Jesus) Matthew 5:17-18

The Voice of Jesus spoke the very universe into existence. This same power is found in the words recorded in the Bible. The Holy Spirit continues to speak into existence new life, healing and restoration in our own lives today through God's Word, the Bible.

By the word of the Lord were the heavens made, their starry host by the breath of his mouth. He gathers the waters of the sea into jars; he puts the deep into storehouses. Let all the earth fear the Lord; let all the people of the world revere him. For he spoke and it came to be; he commanded, and it stood firm. Psalm 33:6-9

In the beginning God created the heavens and the earth. Now the earth was formless and empty, darkness was over the surface of the deep, and the Spirit of God was hovering over the water. And God said, "Let there be light," and there was light. Genesis 1:1-3

By faith we understand that the universe was formed at God's command, so that what is seen was not made out of what was visible. Hebrews 11:3

And we all, who with unveiled faces contemplate the Lord's glory, are being transformed into his image with ever-increasing glory, which comes from the Lord, who is the Spirit. 2 Corinthians 3:18

As we read the Bible, we must urge ourselves over and over to lean more on the Voice of Jesus than our own understanding, surrendering our thoughts to God's thoughts. Our perceptions can easily deceive us, as our thinking and reasoning are strongly influenced by the circumstances of the moment, our fluid emotional state, our overall selfish nature and our unremitting sinful tendencies. In addition, our perceptions are further clouded by the ever-changing environment, culture and opinions of others. For these reasons, the Bible serves as an anchor for our soul, our mind, our spirit and our very lives. We must depend on God's Word holding truer than our own thoughts, feelings, experiences and perceptions. We are but a flash. His Word lasts forever.

I seek you with all my heart; do not let me stray from your commands. I have hidden your word in my heart that I might not sin against you. Psalm 119:10-11

Trust in the Lord with all your heart and lean not on your own understanding; in all your ways acknowledge him and he will make your paths straight. Proverbs 3:5

By relying on the Bible, God's Word, as a source more solid than our own thinking and yet more active than young plants in spring, we permit the Holy Spirit's Voice to reveal more to us, sharpening our ability to hear and detect the ever deepening nuances of the Voice of Jesus. Offer Jesus unlimited entry into your heart and mind and see what God can do in you through His Living Word, the Bible.

For the word of God is living and active. Sharper than any doubled-edged sword, it penetrates even to dividing soul and spirit, joints and marrow; it judges the thoughts and attitudes of the heart.
Hebrews 4:12

Now to him who is able to do immeasurably more than all we ask or imagine, according to his power that is at work within us, to him be glory in the church and in Christ Jesus throughout all generations, for ever and ever! Amen. Ephesians 3:20-21

Why Jesus?

But what about you?" he (Jesus) asked. "Who do you say I am?" Simon Peter answered, "You are the Messiah, the Son of the living God." Matthew 16:15

Jesus is asking each person this same question today, "Who do you say that I am?" To all who will listen, Jesus has already made the answer clear.

Jesus answered, "I am the way and the truth and the life. No one comes to the Father except through me." John 14:6

Christianity is the only faith or worldview in which everything has already been done for the believer. In other faith and belief systems, the person works to reach God. In Christianity, God reached out to us through His Son, Jesus. There is no other person, idea or religion that can save our souls but Jesus. There is no one else. The gift of salvation is freely given. The follower of Jesus need only believe Jesus is the Son of God who died and rose again for our sins and accept the gift of eternal life in Christ. Jesus fulfilled all that was necessary to atone for humanity's sin through his death on the cross. There is nothing anyone can add to this. Instead, believers can only receive, be grateful and out of that unending gratitude, follow Jesus and His teachings recorded in the Bible.

The world will tell you, "Follow your heart." Jesus will tell you, "Follow me." We cannot save ourselves before a Holy God. Only Jesus can save us, but this acceptance requires a humble and penitent heart before Him.

I passed on to you what was most important and what had also been passed on to me. Christ died for our sins, just as the Scriptures said. He was buried, and he was raised from the dead on the third day, just as the Scriptures said. 1 Corinthians 15:3-4 (NLT)

If you declare with your mouth, "Jesus is Lord," and believe in your heart that God raised him from the dead, you will be saved. Romans 10:9

Then Jesus said to his disciples, "Whoever wants to be my disciple must deny themselves and take up their cross and follow me." Matthew 16:24

Jesus knew no sin. He was a perfect sinless sacrifice given up to save humankind from sin. However, the Bible also documents that although Jesus lived a pure life free of any sin, at the same time He did experience every human temptation. Therefore, no matter what temptation, struggle or evil you may be facing in your life, Jesus has suffered that, too. Though he did not fall prey to sin, he did feel our temptations, so he knows the cold, harsh reality of evil and sin and how difficult this life can be.

God made him who had no sin to be sin for us, so that in him we might become the righteousness of God.
2 Corinthians 5:21

For we do not have a high priest who is unable to empathize with our weaknesses, but we have one who has been tempted in every way, just as we are—yet he did not sin. Hebrews 4:15

Jesus is the One who walked this earth in bodily form. Jesus knows how it feels to be betrayed by those closest to you. Jesus was misunderstood, disrespected, wrongfully accused, beaten, spit upon, slapped, whipped and hung on a cross to die. Every earthly pain is one He understands, so Jesus is the friend who sees, knows and understands your pain like no other. Cry to Him, "Jesus it hurts. Jesus it hurts. Jesus it hurts." And listen for His voice, "I know. I know. I am here with you and I cry with you. I see your heart. I see this world. I see every hurt, every tear, every heartache. I know. I know."

He was despised and rejected by men, a man of sorrows and familiar with suffering. Like one from whom men hide their faces he was despised, and we esteemed him not. Surely he took up our infirmities and carried our sorrows, yet we considered him stricken by God, smitten by him, and afflicted. But he was pierced for our transgressions, he was crushed for our iniquities; the punishment that brought us peace was upon him, and by his wounds we are healed.
Isaiah 53:3-5

They went to a place called Gethsemane, and Jesus said to his disciples, "Sit here while I pray." He took Peter, James and John along with him and he began to be deeply distressed and troubled. "My soul is overwhelmed with sorrow to the point of death," he said to them. "Stay here and keep watch." Going a little farther, he fell to the ground and prayed that if possible the hour might pass from him. "Abba, Father," he said, "everything is possible for you. Take this cup from me. Yet not what I will but what you will." Mark 14:32-36

Following His death and resurrection, Jesus ascended into heaven, where He lives and intercedes for us eternally. Though Jesus' earthly suffering is now over, He still sees us where we are in every moment of this life on earth and He prays for us, He intercedes on our behalf. We are on His mind. We are on His heart. We are in His prayers.

Who will bring any charge against those whom God has chosen? It is God who justifies. Who is he that condemns? Christ Jesus, who died – more than that, who was raised to life – is at the right hand of God and is also interceding for us. Romans 8:32-33

Now there have been many of those priests, since death prevented them from continuing in office; but because Jesus lives forever, he has a permanent priesthood. Therefore he is able to save completely those who come to God through him, because he always lives to intercede for them. Hebrews 7:23-25

When we don't know what to say or when the hurt is so deep that we simply have no words, the Holy Spirit, who dwells in the hearts of all believers, will pray for us with sighs and groans that are too deep for words. So, Jesus not only sees our pain and understands our pain, but he prays for us through our pain. Through the Holy Spirit, Jesus becomes our mediator, our intercessor, our counselor, our Voice.

In the same way, the Spirit helps us in our weakness. We do not know what we ought to pray for, but the Spirit himself intercedes for us with groans that words cannot express. And he who searches our hearts knows the mind of the Spirit, because the Spirit intercedes for the saints in accordance with God's will. Romans 8:26-27

Jesus our Savior, Jesus our Friend, Jesus our Voice. Though He was the Son of God, He humbled himself, lived in this painful world and experienced great heartache, abuse and suffering even unto death on a cross. Because Jesus arose from the grave, He is now seated at the right hand of God in heaven interceding, praying for us right now. The Holy Spirit is here with us, helping speak through us, giving us a Voice when we have no voice. Though he was sinless, Jesus experienced every single temptation that we feel, so He understands in a personal way how hard our lives are. He is our way. He is our truth. He is our life. Jesus our Savior, Jesus our Friend, Jesus our Voice.

Section Two

What's Next?
Prepare

SECTION TWO – WHAT'S NEXT? PREPARE

I have the Bible, I have Jesus, what's next?
Prepare, Listen, Write, Pray

Prepare

What do I need?
Bible
Notebook/pencil
Notecards/sticky notes
Time/Space
Mind, heart, spirit, body open to the Holy Spirit
Invitation to the Holy Spirit to speak, teach, comfort, heal, guide, convict, reveal, empower, love

Create a Haven of Time/Schedule/Regularity

Choose a quiet time when you can let the Word of God and Voice of Jesus wash over you, lift you, love you, hold you and ring out over the noise of this world, this chaotic life. The Father, Son and Holy Spirit are gentle and speak in whispers to our souls. God does not push or shout, so if we do not quiet our life, we will not be able to hear the Voice of Jesus over the cacophony of work, chores, family, friends, dishes, laundry, bills.

Carve out a tiny piece of your schedule every single day for you and Jesus. Choose a time that will work on a regular basis, like when you first wake up, when you get home from work, before getting ready for bed or just after mealtimes. You wouldn't consider going through your day without brushing your teeth and hair, taking a shower, getting dressed or putting on shoes. Your time with Jesus is like eating a meal to strengthen your soul. It is a necessity. Absolutely critical for your survival. Your very existence depends upon this time. Be desperate. Be fierce. Be diligent. Find a way.

Create a Haven of Space

Choose a place that will support a peaceful, personal, private quiet time. A place with as few distractions as possible. A place of peace, serenity and calm. A place where you will want to find Jesus and be by yourself with Him. An escape for the soul. It does not need to be beautiful, though you may add beauty to your place with Jesus. The real beauty of that place comes from within as you become more aware of the indwelling Holy Spirit at work in your life. The real beauty of the place comes from the Voice of Jesus painting new scenes on the canvas of your heart. The real beauty of the place comes from the Bible, where the Voice of Jesus will sing a new song over you with words and melodies designed just for you. Some people use a closet for complete privacy. For you it may be a spare room, kneeling by your bedside, a favorite chair or a sunshiny corner of the kitchen. Search for a place that will allow you to be alone with Jesus, as if meeting a dear friend at a small table for two at the local coffee shop. Find a place of comfort that feels like the sweetness of home.

Try to set aside a small area for hanging handwritten Bible verses and prayer responses. These may be on 3x5 cards, sticky notes, or scraps of paper. It is helpful if the Bible verses can remain on display in that place. This way, the Bible verse notecards and prayer response notecards serve as prompts and are ready and in place, maximizing the time spent away in your haven with Jesus.

Come near to God and he will come near to you. James 4:8a

You will seek me and find me when you seek me with all your heart. Jeremiah 29:13

Ask and it will be given to you; seek and you will find; knock and the door will be opened to you. For everyone who asks receives; the one who seeks finds; and to the one who knocks, the door will be opened. (Jesus) Matthew 7:7-8

Which version of the Bible should I read?

Obtain a version of the Bible you can understand. Some examples of the Bible include: New International Version (NIV), New Living Translation (NLT), New King James Version (NKJV), New Revised Standard (NRSV), English Standard Version (ESV), King James Version (KJV), YouVersion (online). Trust the Holy Spirit and the Word of God written in the Bible to be your teacher. God knows you better than anyone else. Jesus loves you enough to die for you. The Holy Spirit is within all believers to draw them near the heart of Jesus. God is all-seeing and all-knowing and wants you to draw near. What teacher could be better than God's Word and the Holy Spirit to instruct you and guide you?

Many Bibles offer a short summary at the beginning of each book. Reading a short summary of a given book of the Bible is helpful as it provides a basic overview and some brief background information so that passages found in that particular book are not accidentally taken out of context or misunderstood. However, avoid lengthy commentaries as then the author may add his/her heart's reflections into your reading. Invite the Word of God and the Holy Spirit to be your greatest teachers.

Where do I start reading in the Bible to find the Voice and Words of Jesus?

If you have never read the Bible before, a good place to begin is the New Testament. The Old Testament tells of God's work with humanity through His chosen people, the Israelites, and the Old Testament foreshadows the coming of Jesus. However, the story of Jesus' life actually begins in the New Testament, so that is the best beginning point.

Start with one of the gospels, Matthew, Mark, Luke or John. These four books are called the gospels because they tell the good news of Jesus. A personal favorite is to begin with the book of John. The book of John tells the story of Jesus, but relates Jesus back to God at the beginning of creation before all time. After reading through the book of John, continue reading through the New Testament.

Next read the book of Psalms. The book of Psalms is like a condensed form of the Bible. It speaks of the sovereignty of God, foretells the coming of Jesus and declares our future eternal home with the Lord in heaven. The Psalms are songs and poems which express a vast range of emotions from the highest praise to the deepest cry.

For those who are already familiar with the Bible you might begin or continue a Bible reading plan to cover a particular topic or to cover the entire Bible within a year. Choose a plan that matches your needs. Regardless of your Bible reading plan, the Bible is Living Water and reading it will renew your heart, so come with a thirsty heart, ready to receive times of refreshing from the Word of God.

Section Three

Listen and Write

SECTION THREE – LISTEN AND WRITE

Listen
Preparing to Pray the Scriptures
Listen and Record the Voice of Jesus from Your Bible Reading

One goal of reading the Bible is to hear God's Voice and get to know Him, His character, His thoughts, His will and His heart. As you spend time reading the Bible you become more familiar with His mind, His Voice and the amazing love He has for you. Reading the Bible allows the God who created you to communicate His Words of love to you. It opens the door to an ongoing conversation and relationship with your Father God, the Creator and Lover of your soul.

The second goal of reading the Bible, in this case, is to collect Bible verses that resonate most deeply and connect with you personally so that you will eventually be able to write your own scripture prayer. As you continue reading the Bible, your collection of heartfelt Bible verses will expand one by one. Once your collection grows large enough, you can then compose a personal scripture prayer by intertwining the Words of Jesus with the cries of your own heart.

When you read the Bible, always begin with a passionate invitation. As you read, every time you read, invite the Holy Spirit to reveal truth from the Bible that will teach you God's ways, remembering that God will meet you where you are at this present moment while simultaneously stretching you toward Himself and His Word. Welcoming the Holy Spirit to be at work before reading prepares your heart and mind for listening. Listening is key!

Keep a notebook nearby whenever you read the Bible. Be ready to take notes! As you read, jot down the scripture references (book, chapter and verses) to gather a list of verses that are meaningful to you. It is not necessary to write out the whole verse in the midst of reading, simply record the references that will allow you to look back later and write it out. There is no need to interrupt the Voice of Jesus by writing out full verses while you are reading. Soak it in. Be comforted. Be touched. Be healed. For now, read, pause, listen and record the verses that teach you, that touch your heart and echo the heartbeats of pain you feel. This is a time for reading, listening, reflecting and healing.

Another effective strategy for discovering verses that speak to your soul is to explore the contents of a book of Bible promises or a Bible concordance, which is an index of Biblical topics found at the back of some Bibles. These resources contain various categories citing specific verses that address a given theme or topic and can be valuable aids helping you mine the passages that will shine like precious gemstones in your spirit. A book of Bible promises or a Bible concordance are two valuable tools that are advantageous for both new and lifelong readers of the Bible. If you are familiar enough with the Bible and can remember phrases or parts of verses that speak to your heart, an additional strategy is to conduct a Bible search on the internet to find the exact verses that will meet your needs. Look for the context surrounding those verses in the given chapter to add understanding.

After reading the Bible and recording the scripture references of verses that teach you, help you or touch your heart, next take a few minutes to write out the complete verse for each scripture reference you have collected in your notebook. As you continue to collect scripture references, keep a running list and add on to it whenever a Bible verse or passage speaks to your heart. Sometimes it can be soothing, while you are reading, to copy the entire verse or passage that expresses your heart, that articulates your sorrow, your dreams and your desires. If so, take the time to allow the Bible to be your Word of comfort from Jesus as you copy down the full verse in your notebook.

Once you have recorded in your notebook and written out the verses that resonate with your heart, next select the specific verses you want to include in your scripture prayer. Recopy the selected verses from your notebook onto notecards or sticky notes. Include the scripture references so you know where the verses are located in the Bible if you want to look back for contextual meaning.

What Should My Scripture Prayer Include?

God sees all, knows all and has collected every single tear that has fallen from your heart. So your scripture prayer can be designed around the Bible verses that connect with your heart. Ask the Holy Spirit to lead you to the verses you need to compose the prayer of your soul, spoken through the Voice of Jesus.

As a point of reference, these are some elements to consider for your scripture prayer.

Praise and Thanksgiving
Approach the beginning of any prayer with a sense of who God is and what He has done, so that you can remember how big God is and how great is His love in comparison to the problems we bring before Him.

Confession
Ask God to reveal to you the secret sins and hidden pride of your own heart, so that you can approach the Lord with a pure and sincere heart, clear of deceit. Tell God you are sorry and ask His forgiveness for the times you have failed by rebelling against His Word or hurting others or yourself. When we are honest with God and ourselves, His forgiveness makes our hearts lighter and we can communicate more freely.

Requests for Self, Loved Ones or the World
God cares about every detail of your life, so you can pray about anything. *~Cast all your anxiety on him because he cares for you. 1 Peter 5:7~*

Our Heavenly Father cares about all of your worries, sorrows, hopes and dreams. However, more than earthly blessings, He longs to be close to you, just you. Therefore, when offering prayer requests for self, loved ones or the world, try to let your heart pursue spiritual blessings, more so than worldly blessings. For example, praying for someone to draw closer to God, to surrender their lives fully to Jesus and His Word as found in the Bible, to have their heart be opened to a revelation of our Sovereign God, Savior Jesus, Holy Spirit; these are all spiritual blessings that will last for all eternity. When requesting earthly things like a new relationship, a new house, a new job, even for our health, these are all temporary blessings and when we pray for these we are praying for the lesser things. When bringing prayer requests to God, let us fix our eyes on Jesus and run hard toward Him in our prayers. Anything less is settling for an inferior and temporary pleasure as compared to the lasting beauty and magnificence of Jesus' Presence in our lives.

Promises of God/Faith Strengthening
A powerful way to end a prayer is with Bible verses of God's promises and verses that strengthen your faith. This way, you have opened and closed your prayer time with the fullness of God.

Write
Writing Prayers Using Scripture

For each scripture notecard you have prepared, write a short sentence prayer to express that verse in your own words. The Bible verse will be written on one notecard and the corresponding prayer will be written on another notecard and eventually organized into a complete personal scripture prayer.

Sample:
Bible Verse - *Romans 5:8 – For God demonstrates his own love for us in this, while we were still sinners, Christ died for us.*
Corresponding Prayer – Thank you Father, that while I was still in rebellion against you, you loved me so much you sent your own Son, Jesus, to save me. I didn't deserve such love. It's only because of Your big heart.

Once your scripture notecards and prayer response notecards are complete, post each scripture verse on a wall or door in your special place, your haven with Jesus. Post the corresponding prayer notecard underneath or beside the scripture notecard. This allows your scripture prayer to flow easily from one Bible verse to the next based on the verses you have selected and the responsive prayers you have written.

Now it's time! Use the scriptures you have collected to write your own scripture prayer. May the words of Jesus, found in the Bible, be your voice in the night.

Sample Scripture Prayer

The following is a sample scripture prayer that includes the suggested elements: Praise, Thanksgiving, Confession, Requests, Promises of God and Faith Strengthening Verses.

Scripture - Psalm 93:1-2
The LORD reigns, he is robed in majesty; the LORD is robed in majesty and armed with strength; indeed, the world is established, firm and secure. Your throne was established long ago; you are from all eternity.
Prayer – Dear God, You are above all. You are majestic and powerful. You are the Creator of this earth and You hold everything in place through your mighty strength. You are eternal and Your kingdom lasts forever. I praise You, my God.

Scripture - John 3:16-17
For God so loved the world that he gave his one and only Son, that whoever believes in him shall not perish but have eternal life. For God did not send his Son into the world to condemn the world, but to save the world through him.
Prayer – Thank you, Lord, that you loved everyone so much to give up Your own precious Son, Jesus, so that you could save us. Thank you, Jesus, for giving up your life for me. I am humbled by such deep love. No one else could ever love me as much as You.

Scripture – 1 John 1:9
If we confess our sins, he is faithful and just and will forgive us our sins and purify us from all unrighteousness.
Prayer – Father, forgive me for the sins and wrongs I have done. Expose areas of my heart that are in need of Your changing. Help me be honest with You and with myself about my faults. Give me a humble heart and a pure heart before You.

Scripture - Isaiah 55:6
Seek the LORD while he may be found; call on him while he is near.
Prayer – Lord, give me a heart to seek after You with all my strength. Let me desire to be near You more than I desire anything else.

Scripture - Jeremiah 31:3
I have loved you with an everlasting love; I have drawn you with unfailing kindness.
Prayer – Father, I lift up my loved ones. Draw them close to Your heart with Your everlasting love and kindness. Help them to love You, too.

Scripture - Ephesians 6:10
Be strong in the Lord and in his mighty power.
Prayer – Holy Spirit, fill my loved ones and me with Your power so that we can live more fully for you. Fill us with Your love, Your truth, Your wisdom and the strength that only comes from You.

Scripture - 2 Corinthians 5:17
Therefore, if anyone is in Christ, the new creation has come: The old has gone, the new is here!
Prayer – Jesus, create in my loved ones and me a new heart. Transform every part of us to be brand new in You. Where we are broken or hurting, heal us, Father.

Scripture - Exodus 14:14
The LORD will fight for you; you need only to be still.
Prayer – Almighty God, fight for me with Your power. Let me rest in You.

Scripture - Deuteronomy 33:27a
The eternal God is your refuge, and underneath are the everlasting arms.
Prayer – Everlasting Father, let me remember that You are my hiding place. When everything else around me falls, Your love will last forever. I place myself in Your strong and loving arms.

Scripture - Matthew 9:13b
For I have not come to call the righteous, but sinners.
Prayer – Thank you, Jesus, that you didn't come for perfect people, but you came to save people like me who are broken, dirty, rebellious and sinful.

Scripture - Matthew 18:14
In the same way your Father in heaven is not willing that any of these little ones should perish.
Prayer – Thank you, Heavenly Father, that your heart's desire is that all would be with you in heaven.

Scripture - Jeremiah 32:17
Ah, Sovereign LORD, you have made the heavens and the earth by your great power and outstretched arm. Nothing is too hard for you.
Prayer – Lord, you are Sovereign and all powerful. Nothing is too difficult for you. You can do anything.

Scripture - Matthew 19:26
Jesus looked at them and said, "With man this is impossible, but with God all things are possible."
Prayer – God, thank you that you can do things we cannot. You can do the impossible.

Scripture - Matthew 28:20
Lo, I am with you always, even to the end of the age.
Prayer – Thank you, Jesus, for coming to this earth, to die for me. Thank you, that through your Holy Spirit, you will be with me and within me from now until eternity. I am never alone.

~~~*~~~

Section Four

What's Next?
Pray

SECTION FOUR – WHAT'S NEXT? PRAY

Pray With Your Body, Mind and Spirit

You have collected Bible verses that mirror your heart's cry. You have selected specific verses to include in your prayer. You have written personal sentence prayers that reflect each verse in your scripture prayer collection. You have assembled your scripture verses and prayer response cards into a complete prayer. Now you are ready to begin praying the Voice of Jesus. Using the time already set aside to meet with Jesus, continue to spend time meeting with Him in your haven of space. Bring all the strength of your mind. We often hear the phrase, "be mindful". Bringing our thoughts, our focus and all the strength of our will into captivity before Jesus is critical. Let Jesus captivate your mind!

In addition to being mindful, consider being "heartful". Let the Holy Spirit shine a flashlight into the corners of your heart to see what is hidden there. Let that light cast a ray of sunshine from God's heart into yours. Remember God loves you, Jesus loves you and the Holy Spirit was sent to guide you. Begin where you are. Why are you hurting? What is involved in the pain you feel? Ask the Holy Spirit to help you examine all the broken pieces of your heart to bring the healing you need. Welcome the Holy Spirit to speak to you, to open your eyes and mind to pray through the Bible verses allowing Jesus to speak to your pain and through your pain. Jesus knows about pain. You can turn to Him. He will cry with you. In addition to being called the Comforter, the Holy Spirit is also called, the Counselor. Allow the Holy Spirit to bring comfort and Godly counseling to your whole being.

You keep track of all my sorrows. You have collected all my tears in your bottle. You have recorded each one in your book. Psalm 56:8 (NLT)

For to us a child is born, to us a son is given, and the government will be on his shoulders. And he will be called Wonderful Counselor, Mighty God, Everlasting Father, Prince of Peace. Isaiah 9:6

Bring not only your mind and heart, but also your whole body to your time with Jesus. Breathe deeply. Breathe slowly. Fill your lungs with the breath of life that was given to you by your loving Creator. Remind yourself that God created you and knows every part of you, sees every need and longs for you to draw near. Think back to the love of the Father, that He gave His one and only Son to save you. Remember the love of Jesus, willing to go to the ends of the earth and back to save you. Press into this love. Let it wrap around you like a blanket.

Choose a body position that is open, awake, relaxed and ready to receive. Do not lie down, as this too easily leads to sleeping. Try standing, kneeling, sitting, walking a few paces back and forth, swaying. You may choose to lift your hands to Him, change positions or move in worshipful ways as you pray. Choose physical positions that enable and encourage you to remain awake, alert, alive and ready to receive from the Holy Spirit. Imagine a close friend sitting across from you at the table as you share a meal. How would you demonstrate your attentiveness? Be attentive to God with your body. Having mounted the Bible verse and prayer notecards on a wall or door facilitates hands-free, physically active, movement oriented prayer. Pray with your body, mind and spirit, all of who God created you to be.

You have fully prepared for your prayer time. You have prepared notecards with the Bible verses that address your heartache and short sentence prayer notecards that reflect each verse. You have hung the verse and prayer cards in your haven of space. You have brought all the strength of your being. You are ready to continue the process of praying with your body, mind and spirit using your own personal scripture prayer.

Pray Aloud the Words of Jesus

When you pray, speak aloud the Bible verses and sentence prayers you have written. Say them out loud, listening to the sound of your own voice. If you are concerned about being overheard, use a whisper voice. **At all costs, avoid praying in your mind!** Praying silently in your mind allows your mind to wander too easily. Speak aloud. Speaking or whispering aloud helps maintain your focus. Speaking or whispering aloud while praying, is also another way to involve your whole body, as well as your mind and spirit. Praying aloud adds the physical modality of speaking and hearing as you pray, to further engage all parts of who God created you to be as a human being. Body, mind and spirit.

Love the Lord your God with all your heart and with all your soul and with all your mind and with all your strength. (Jesus) Mark 12:30

Slowly read aloud the Bible verse recorded on each notecard. Allow each verse to pour from Jesus' heart to yours. Pause after each verse and listen for the Holy Spirit to illuminate His Word so it can reach the farthest corners of your mind and heart. Let the meaning soak in. Absorb God's Truth with a deep soulful understanding. As you pause in stillness, the Holy Spirit may remind you of another scripture verse or to bring to mind a song or a memory of God's love from your past that carries a similar message allowing the meaning of this verse to shine even more brightly into the dark corners of your present circumstances.

Follow the reading of each Bible verse by reading aloud your prayer response written on the corresponding prayer notecard. Read the prayer notecard slowly with expression, putting your whole heart into the words. Let the words of your heart ring out. Pause again and wait for the Holy Spirit to move in your heart bringing a sense of Jesus' Presence with you. You may feel all has been said or you may now think of additional verbal prayer responses to add to your written prayer. Allow the Holy Spirit to work in you, bringing comfort, healing, faith and hope. Invite the Holy Spirit to bring a sense of God's presence, God's power, God's goodness, God's forgiveness and God's deep abiding love for you. Voice of Jesus, pray for me.

How Much Time is Needed?

Time. Give yourself the gift of time. Your life story cannot be illustrated by a single hastily scribbled sketch or quick one-shot selfie, but instead is made up of a series of countless, various events flowing from one moment to the next over the span of a day, week, month, year and lifetime. As we look back over our lives and then look ahead to the future, we know the best part is yet to come for those who believe in Jesus! We are assured of a wonderful ending awaiting us at the conclusion of our life story, as we join our Savior Jesus in heaven. In the meantime, our best hope is to pursue Jesus as each scene from the movie of our lives unfolds in the here and now and rejoice as the Lord moves with us through each chapter.

Like the rest of life, sorrow and grief are not captured in a single snapshot and then tucked away into a drawer, stored out of sight and out of mind. Sorrow and grief are teachers and their lessons are difficult, their assignments long-term, their syllabus hidden from view. Look at this experience as a journey and remind yourself that Jesus is with you every step of the way, feeling your pain, seeing your tears, reaching with arms outstretched saying, "I know, I know." God wants to be more than a once-upon-a-time experience where you cry out, then dry your eyes, slap band-aids on your knees, start running by yourself again and never look back at God. God is your Creator, your heavenly Father, your Savior. Out of His heart of love for you, He sent Jesus. Tell yourself, "He loves me, He loves me, He loves me." Jesus wants to be your closest friend, your friend who sticks closer than a brother, even in the darkest of hours.

One who has unreliable friends soon comes to ruin, but there is a friend who sticks closer than a brother. Proverbs 18:24

The more time and space you allow for Jesus, the more opportunity you give Him to love you. Let Him love you. Jesus is waiting. He wants to come into your heart, your mind, your pain, your every day, your every moment. Let Him in. Let Jesus love you. Oh, how He loves you.

If we pour out the sorrows of life to a friend, we would expect them to check back in with us periodically to see how we are doing. A friendship means repeated conversations day after day. We enjoy the company of friends and want to visit with them time and time again, sharing thoughts and feelings and experiencing life together. We want to talk and laugh and be close. Good times and bad times. We want to share it all.

Having a relationship with God is no different. Open your heart to Him. Set aside time every day to draw near to Him. Ask the Holy Spirit to seep more and more deeply into your heart and mind. Ask Him to open your eyes to see His hand at work in the morning sunrise, in the soft touch of a kitten, in the warm smile of a co-worker. Ask Him to transform your heart into the heart of a seeker. Seek Him with all your heart, soul, mind and strength. Spend time every single day reading His Word, the Bible, so you can hear the Voice of Jesus more and more. Set a goal of reading the Bible and praying for 15 minutes every single day. Increase that amount of time as you are able. Would you spend any less time communicating with those closest to you? Compare your screen time or time spent on social media with your time spent with Jesus. Doesn't the Friend who died for you deserve this much and even more?

Treasure this most precious relationship with the One who created you and loves you like no other. This relationship is a remarkable gift. In the Old Testament, only the high priest was afforded such close access to Almighty God because of God's great holiness, purity, goodness and powerful Presence. In our mere earthly mortal bodies, we simply cannot behold One who is so far beyond and above us. Imagine yourself standing at the edge of the ocean as the immense waves crash on your feet. The weight, power and magnificence contained in this ocean cannot be fully explained in words, but instead must be sensed and experienced, as in the deep places of your soul. This is only a tiny glimpse of the immeasurable magnitude and force behind our powerful Lord who with the sheer sound of His Voice spoke all of creation into being. We are but a grain of sand in the face of such enormity. Thankfully, through the blood sacrifice of His Son Jesus, the way has now been opened for us to have access and draw near to our Holy Lord God like never before. Cherish this sacred closeness with the Maker and Lover of your soul.

Be willing to give Jesus time. He made you. He knows you. He loves you. He is waiting for you. No appointment needed. What other friend is always waiting for you? Jesus is waiting, always waiting.

Closing - "The Gift of Pain"

If you have never asked Jesus to be the Lord of your life and you want to do that now, here is a simple prayer you can say. "Jesus, I believe you are the Son of God who came to earth to die for my sins and who then rose again. I know I am a sinner and I am sorry for all the things I have done wrong. Please forgive me for my sins and come into my heart today. Be my Savior and the Lord of my life. I want to live for You and follow Your truth as written in the Bible. I love you. Amen."

If you are holding this book in your hands, reading these words, know this, it is not an accident. You are not forgotten. Jesus is drawing you near to His heart. Jesus loves you. Jesus is praying for you. Jesus will be with you, praying you through your situation, not around it, but through it. Remember you were not made for this world of sorrow, pain, suffering and evil. You were made for much more. You were made for an eternal life in heaven with the Lord of love, where there will be no more death, no more sorrow, no more tears, no more pain.

Jesus suffered great pain to give us this eternal gift. So, He knows the cost of pain and the price of love.

I consider that our present sufferings are not worth comparing with the glory that will be revealed in us. Romans 8:18

He will wipe every tear from their eyes. There will be no more death or mourning or crying or pain, for the old order of things has passed away. Revelation 21:4

The greatest gifts God could ever give while we live here on earth are the gift of life in His beautiful creation, the gift of His Living Word, the Bible, the gift of His very own Son, Jesus, and the gift of His very own Presence, the Holy Spirit. Through Jesus, His Word and His Holy Spirit in our lives, we get a glimpse of God's glory, a glimpse of heaven. Voice of Jesus, draw us near through our deepest pain, give us the gift of Your Presence, Your Holy Spirit. If suffering draws you near to Jesus, remind yourself, you have found the greatest peace and fulfillment there will ever be this side of heaven. Enjoy the all-surpassing joy of knowing Jesus and loving Jesus, not after your pain and hardships are over, but right here, right now in the midst of your pain and sorrow. All other relationships and earthly experiences pale in comparison to a feast shared in your heart with Jesus, the Bread of Life. Time spent with Jesus becomes more than time. Time spent with Jesus becomes an eternal flash we are afforded in this fleeting life, as His never-ending rays of love cast their light into our momentary fading darkness. Time spent with Jesus provides a taste of eternity as our rapidly evaporating days intersect with His infinite love, transforming one twinkling moment into thousands and thousands of timeless years of sweet, heavenly love. In view of this, though tears streak our faces, our still cracking voices can rise and sing, "In dark of night when words fail, Voice of Jesus, pray for me."

Only in the hands of God then, can pain become a gift. But in the hands of God, so it does.

It was just before the Passover Festival. Jesus knew that the hour had come for him to leave this world and go to the Father. Having loved his own who were in the world, he loved them to the end. John 13:1

ACKNOWLEDGEMENTS

I wish to express my deepest gratitude to the following people:

Macedonia Ministries family, for helping me run harder to know and love God and His Word, the Bible.

Ministers Donald and Precious Graham, for the inspiration, wise counsel and encouragement.

Dr. Jules and Laurel Casseus of North Haiti Christian University, for your loving guidance, mentoring, prayers and Christ-like lives.

Dr. Louima Lilite of Oklahoma Baptist University, for your wisdom, kindness, inspired writing, Spirit-filled music and unshakable faith in Jesus.

My brothers, Chris and Jon, and my whole family, for supporting and loving me through each season.

My parents, Raymond and Marty Miller, for telling me about Jesus, raising me to love Him and living like Him in ways small and large.

My three children, Shannon, Laurel and Chris, precious gifts from God above, for all your love and support from the start.

My beloved husband, Tom McLaughlin, for the beautiful cover design, the beauty you create in my world, the beauty of Christ you have taught me and shown me.

Every person who has helped me to love Jesus and His Word, the Bible. I am forever grateful.

To my Lord and Savior, Jesus Christ, the One who saved me and loves me like no other.